SHORT STEPS
to a foreign language

Stephen Hernandez

Copyright © 2021 by Stephen Hernandez

All rights reserved. No part of this publication may be reproduced, distributed or transmitted in any form or by any means, without prior written permission.

www.stephenhernandez.co.uk

Publisher's Note: This is a work of non-fiction. Locales and public names are sometimes used for atmospheric purposes. Any resemblance to actual people, living or dead, or to businesses, companies, events, institutions, or locales is completely coincidental unless otherwise stated

Book Layout © 2017 BookDesignTemplates.com

Easy Steps - to a foreign language/ Stephen Hernandez. -- 1st ed.

Dedicated to Isabelle

A new language is a new life.

—PERSIAN PROVERB

CONTENTS

Introduction	P7
1. Learning a foreign language	P12
2. Learning on your own	P20
3. Practicing on your own	P28
4. Short steps for learning	P32
5. Why speaking beats grammar every time	P38
6. Motivation and the complete beginner	P47
7. Fluency	P51
8. Learning like a child	P66
9. Short steps to speaking a foreign language	P71

INTRODUCTION

How often have you heard the phrase "Anything worth doing is hard?" Whenever I struggled in something, I would complain, "Do I really need to do this? What's the point?" And of course, someone would respond by telling me something along the lines of everything worthwhile is difficult. It seemed as if I was supposed to take pride in hardship. Hard work, after all, is seen as a necessary evil to get anywhere.

Maybe people are right. To get good at anything, you have to be willing to do what most people won't. You need to be willing to persist for a long time before you see results. But I still couldn't help myself from thinking about what that phrase meant—anything worth doing is hard. Is hard work in itself valuable? What fits into the definition of being worthwhile?

Does the fact that something is difficult to master mean that it's worth doing? After all, some people work long hours with barely any results to show for it. Plus, we only have a limited amount of mental resources. Dedicating ourselves to one project means that we take away the energy that could be spent working on something else.

Let's go over two common misconceptions when it comes to putting in the work.

If something seems too easy, there must be something wrong with the method.

We get skeptical when we hear of an easier way to solve a problem. Sometimes, our feelings are justified. An advertisement that promises instant weight loss will send up red flags in our head. But many times, it's worth reconsidering our current strategy. If we've been doing the same thing over and over, hoping to get a different result, isn't it worth taking a step back and evaluating what has—and hasn't—worked?

So why do we do it? Why do we resist taking the easier route and make things harder on ourselves? It's usually because of one or more of these reasons:

- We want to prove to ourselves that we are capable.

- Finding an advantage seems unfair.

- We want to do something different for the sake of being "innovative."

There are certain ideas about success that hinder our progress. One of them is the idea of fairness. Since an early age, we're led to believe that if each person puts in the same amount of work, each person will generally get the same level of results.

Of course, things aren't so clear in the real world. If you've applied for a competitive position, you know that getting hired can be incredibly difficult, or it can be very easy. More often than not, getting a position depends on who you know. Yet many people resist this idea.

The next time you resist using a strategy that can get you from A to B, consider the source of your skepticism. Is the solution too good to be true, or are your internal beliefs holding you back?

A task must be worth doing because its difficult.

Do you ever feel motivated to complete a challenge that someone presents to you? The gears in your head start to turn, and you think to yourself, "I can do that!"

Smart and ambitious people often fall into this trap. When they see a problem, they want to tackle it and set things straight—or at least try to—even if it's not worth dealing with at all.

Often, we waste our time on something that's unimportant. We might not even take the time to evaluate what we need to do. Just because there's a problem doesn't mean it needs solving.

So before you attempt to solve a problem next time, instead of asking yourself how to solve it; ask yourself *should* you solve it. If you spend time upfront answering the latter question, you'll give yourself the opportunity to put your efforts where they're best used.

While it's true that things worth achieving are difficult, the reverse—difficult goals are worth achieving—isn't always true.

Yes, anything worthwhile will not be easy. There will be obstacles. But sometimes there are ways to circumvent the most difficult aspects by asking for help, studying what someone else did or answering whether you should be solving the problem in the first place.

So first ask, "Is this a problem I need to solve?" And if it is, what's the best way to do so? You don't need to be the smartest person in the room. You don't need to reinvent the wheel. Sometimes a simpler approach will get you to the same destination. Just take a short step...

When it comes to learning a new skill there is one overriding change in learning that began in the twentieth century and that is the use of the Internet.

The Internet is the most awesome learning resource there has ever been. Yet incredibly there are still people who do not use it to gain a new skill, jump start their career or simply pick up a new hobby or interest.

Is it because it seems too easy and in some case it is seen as cheating?

Unfortunately, many people are still stuck with the archaic idea that in order to learn "properly" you need to attend formal classes supervised by a teacher. In some cases this may be true, but as many people will tell you, including those young enough to be taught at home during "lockdown," you can attend virtual classes online and be supervised by a real teacher from your own home.

Learning using the Internet should no longer be considered the second best alternative. For those of us who wish to have a flexible and cost-efficient method of learning any given subject for whatever reason it should be considered the first post of call.

It is just a short step to a world of opportunity.

Take it...

Note: Throughout this book there are hyperlinks to further learning resources. If you are reading in an e-book format, using a Kindle for example, these will appear underlined in blue and clicking them will take you directly to the webpage via a new window. In the paperback version these will appear merely underlined but I have also where possible put the full link in brackets. If this has not been possible because the link has proved too lengthy please Google the source material and I am sure you will find the resource.

CHAPTER ONE

LEARNING A FOREIGN LANGUAGE

Learning a language when you are not living in a country where it is spoken is very difficult. Not only do you not have situations where you can practice your new found learning but you are constantly bombarded by your native language as soon as you leave the classroom or your chosen place of learning.

In many ways it becomes a case of perseverance. I liken it to the starting of a new exercise regime. You enroll in a local gym (giving you the added incentive that you are actually paying to get fitter). At first you are full of enthusiasm and energy so you set yourself unrealistic goals. Instead of starting off walking and progressing to running, you start off at a mad sprint and quickly tire. The novelty soon wears off and going to the gym becomes an irksome duty. Then excuses for not going begin to kick in, and before you know it you have given up altogether

To start off with don't set yourself unrealistic goals or a grandiose study plan. Keep it simple. Set aside a small amount of time that you can reasonably spare even if it just means getting up 15 minutes earlier in the morning. If you set that time aside and avoid distractions that 15 minutes will be invaluable. Above all make it as fun as possible. No one said learning a new language was easy but neither should it be irksome.

This book can be used by itself or in conjunction with other learning resources you may be using.

There are two major techniques used in autodidacticism (self-directed learning) that can aid you in learning a foreign language:

SMART goals and **metacognitive strategies**.

SMART, in this case, is an acronym that means Specific, Measurable, Achievable, Results, Time-bound. The synopsis of this is that you need to make really, really concrete goals that can be achieved. Setting realistic goals like this is an essential skill for anyone studying by themselves, as well as anyone who wishes to maximize their study time.

Metacognitive strategies involves three steps. First, you plan. Ask yourself what your specific goals are and what strategies you're going to use to achieve them. Second, start learning and keep track of how well you do every day. Are you having problems that need new solutions? Write that down. Are you consistently succeeding or failing in a certain area? Keep track of that, too. And the third and final step, after a few weeks to a month, it is time to evaluate yourself. Were you able to achieve your goals? If not, why? What strategies did and didn't work? Then the whole process repeats again.

These two techniques naturally fit together quite well, and they're both indispensable for making sure you're cooking with gas every time you prepare to study.

Tips for efficient self-learning

It has never been easier to self-study in the history of humankind. Beginning your college education, or picking up a new skill has become as simple as googling and signing up for courses. The lessons can be delivered right to your email account, with reminders and additional tools to complete them successfully.

Alternatively, if you do not require a recognized qualification you do not have to sign up for a course at all and can find many of the necessary educational tools and resources online for free.

Throughout this book you will find all the links, tips and recommendations you could ever wish to learn a foreign language of your choice.

The e-learning industry is expected to top the charts off for a value of $325 billion by 2025. This rapid and steady growth is almost entirely due to the number of people who are eager to advance. It is not only students who invest in self-learning programs, but professionals and companies who are looking to train and expand their employees' prowess.

Despite having this myriad of opportunities at the tap of fingers, finding motivation, and managing time is not everyone's cup of tea. Many fall short when it comes to efficiently teaching themselves a new skill or studying any emerging developments in a particular field.

Most individuals are expected to practice independent study right from high school. Whether it is from an online platform or a library, learning on one's own requires commitment and disciple. This applies to everyone, irrespective of age or background.

If you are not sure what kind of learning style you have take the quiz here: https://www.citylit.ac.uk/

Then see what methods suit you best.

Self-Evaluate

Before you initiate an independent study, it is most beneficial to conduct a self-evaluation of your habits. Look at your current situation, lifestyle, family, and support system that you have.

If you have previously failed to keep up with lessons or deadlines, note those incidents and try to avoid such situations.

Look at the concept of self-studying as inspirational rather than something you are forced to do.

The Environment

Having a dedicated study space is a must. From now on you need to consider yourself a professional student and this space will be your office. Keep it sacred and teach others to respect it in the same way.

Studying would be most effective when you stop procrastinating, straighten your spine, and focus on the task at hand. This does not necessarily mean that a desk is the only place where you can learn new things.

The key is to find a comfortable place where you can freely access, analyze, and memorize new data.

Go here to learn about the psychology of learning environments: https://www.educause.edu/research-and-publications/books/learning-spaces

If your mind is able to associate this space with learning, you will be better prepared for any task.

Set Goals

When you are working on each assignment yourself, it can be hard to find encouragement. Setting goals can be a positive way to tackle this issue and self-motivate. Whether you choose daily, weekly, or monthly goals, when you achieve each, the sense of accomplishment will drive you to continue.

According to goal-setting experts Edwin Locke and Gary Latham, goals have to be specific rather than ambiguous. "Do my best" is not definite; on the other hand, "finish these two chapters" will certainly result in a better outcome. These control systems will bring in more efficiency and competence to push oneself.

Goal setting app (www.kapow.life)

The Learning Process

The self-evaluation part becomes ever more significant in implementing the actual learning strategy. Depending on the subject or preference, it is also necessary to establish a study pattern. One can choose a deep approach that is ideal for self-learning as it aims at a better grasp of a subject through examples and applications.

A surface approach, on the other hand, focuses more on studying definitions or translations. The third way is to have a strategic approach to look at the final goal, such as passing exams (if you are learning to further your career).

12 Best Self-Evaluation apps (www.getapp.com)

Assess Learning

As there is no one else to direct or evaluate you, self-learners will have to do the testing themselves. There is no shortage of mock tests or sample papers online to practice and perfect your learning methods.

Although considered time-consuming, the activity can increase the interest and motivation of learners. It also leads to better academic performance and enhanced study outcomes.

[Language proficiency tests (transparent.com)](transparent.com)

Finding the Time

Managing time and staying productive are integral parts of self-learning. Losing focus or getting distracted while studying is not uncommon.

Having a schedule or a proper plan for studying will help to set apart some time every day to concentrate on the activity. It could be trickier if you are a professional to adopt a schedule after a long day at work.

By maintaining a consistent schedule for a few days, you will soon be looking forward to the challenge. Spruce up your study sessions by using visual aids, color-coded calendars, or any one of the hundreds of apps available to help you stay focused.

[18 Best Time Management Apps & Tools (www.lifehack.org)](www.lifehack.org)

Partner Up

Self-learning does not have to be a lonely process. Getting someone to hold you accountable, check upon the progress will make it easier to meet the goals.

You can study separately from the partner, discussing interesting topics, and motivating each other along the way. Additionally, it will urge both parties to find time and energy.

Partnering with someone also gives you the opportunity to teach, further enhancing the knowledge on the subject. One can also consider this as a way of getting feedback. While some online education platforms allow you to get feedback directly, those who do not have this option could always use the help of a partner.

How to find a Language Exchange Partner (https://www.fluentu.com/blog/find-a-language-exchange-partner/)

CHAPTER TWO

LEARNING ON YOUR OWN

Here are 5 amazing strategies to help you learn by yourself that you will not have heard of:

1. Prioritize One Phrase a Day

Resist the urge to cram! Cramming is not only ineffective in the long run, but it's also a poor way to be using your time and energy. (This is exactly why SRS was created for effective learning with flashcards).

Instead of trying to memorize the most words and phrases in short amounts of time, try the reverse. Choose one phrase a day and commit to it.

Some phrases to consider:

- Excuse me, where can I find the nearest bathroom?
- What time do you wake up in the morning?
- My favorite hobbies are writing and playing video games.

Notice how all of these phrases are jam-packed with useful words, while also being incredibly practical.
After you've selected a phrase, devote an entire day to using that phrase as much as you can. Have fun and be creative when trying to implement your daily phrase. By using the phrase repeatedly and focusing your mental energy on it, your brain will have no choice but to let it stick.

The next day, choose a new phrase to focus on, and repeat the process. Within a few weeks, you will have a useful portfolio of words and phrases that you'll have a hard time forgetting. And if you do happen to have trouble remembering your daily phrases, stick with the same phrase for three days, or for an entire week!

If you're stumped on ways to learn such phrases, give these resources a shot:

- Google Translate (translate.google.com) is generally a reliable go-to (but be aware the sentence structure may not be 100% accurate).
- Post your desired translation on an online language learning forum, like Word Reference, (http://www.wordreference.com) so that a native speaker can give you feedback on the proper translation.

2. Closed Caption Your Favorite YouTube Videos

Closed captioning (http://youtu.be/V2cBTlLCKjU) is becoming an increasingly popular option for YouTube content creators. To make the site more appealing to various culture and demographics, YouTube is encouraging viewers to caption videos in other languages. This is a wonderful chance for the site's content to be more universal, and also a great opportunity for you to learn new languages!

If you have a favorite YouTuber who you religiously watch, go back to some of his/her videos and turn on the captions. You can do this by clicking the "CC" button alongside the bottom of the video. Then, click the gear icon located next to the "CC" button to adjust the language. While on this screen, you can also adjust the speed, allowing you to make the video slower so that you can follow along more easily.

Try this with a video in your target language: Listen to only the first sentence and hit pause. From here, see if you know what was said, and then check by re-watching with the English captions. Continue listening and pausing the video, going sentence by sentence.

You can also try to imitate a native speaker by memorizing part of the YouTube video. This allows you to match your native language with the language spoken throughout the video. Try to pick out commonly used words or expressions. You never know what you'll discover!

And if you want to learn a language with videos, but are looking for more than just subtitles, head over to FluentU (fluentu.com).

FluentU takes real-world videos—like music videos, movie trailers, news and inspiring talks—and turns them into personalized language learning lessons.

With FluentU, you hear languages in real-world contexts—the way that native speakers actually use them.

FluentU really takes the grunt work out of learning languages, leaving you with nothing but engaging, effective and efficient learning. It's already hand-picked the best videos for you and organized them by level and topic. All you have to do is choose any video that strikes your fancy to get started.

Each word in the interactive captions comes with a definition, audio, image, example sentences and more.

Access a complete interactive transcript of every video under the Dialogue tab, and easily review words and phrases from the video under Vocab.

You can use FluentU's unique adaptive quizzes to learn the vocabulary and phrases from the video through fun questions and exercises. Just swipe left or right to see more examples of the word you're studying.

The program even keeps track of what you're learning and tells you exactly when it's time for review, giving you a 100% personalized experience.

Start using the FluentU website on your computer or tablet or, better yet, download the FluentU app from the iTunes store or Google Play store.

3. Turn Your Phone into a Language-learning Tool

Admit it. You're already on your phone way more than you should be every day, so why not use the time on your cell to bump up your language learning? Change your phone's language setting to the desired language you would like to learn.

Now, the next time you instinctively check your phone, you'll have the added challenge of deciphering your way through different screens and apps. It definitely gets easier over time, which only means one thing— that you're becoming more comfortable in your target language because you've learned new words.

But we can take it a step up. If you have a smartphone that has a built-in operator feature (i.e. Siri), try speaking to the robot in your new language. This can be a really fun way to test your pronunciation, and an even more fun way to befriend a robot.

If you're really adventurous, try using your GPS wherever you go to hear the directions in that language. When I lived in Rome, being able to navigate myself around the city was crucial. Almost everyday, I found myself either asking for directions or telling a driver directions in Italian. By practicing with your phone's built-in GPS, or even the one in your car, you can easily create a roadmap to success in your language learning endeavors. Thanks technology!

4. Join a Meetup Group of Other Language Learners

Although it may be tempting to learn your new language solo, having a group of like-minded people to support you in your learning can be the make-or-break in your strive for fluency.

Meetup.com is the world's largest network of local groups. By becoming a member, you can easily organize a local group or find one of the thousands already meeting up face-to-face. More than 9,000 groups get together in local communities each day, each one with the goal of improving themselves or their communities.

Currently, there are over 420,000 monthly meetups occurring in 180 countries. Chances are there are many happening in or around your hometown, so give it a shot. You may be able to find a group of other passionate language learners nearby, or you can be the first to get a group started.

With this group, you can share language learning resources, inspire and motivate each other, watch films in your target language, eat at ethnic restaurants where your target language is spoken—and probably gain a few new friends along the way!

5. Stop Trying to Motivate Yourself and Instead Just Go for It

Here's the thing: We have the concept of motivation totally wrong. We tend to believe that first we have to motivate ourselves in order to accomplish or do anything. Before we know it, we sit around all day trying to think of ways to motivate ourselves, and in the process we get nothing done!

It's time we flip the script on how motivation really works. Rather than motivating yourself until you take action, take action until you are motivated. Just the act of doing *something* towards your goal eventually fosters motivation—it's incredible how well it works.

Imagine both motivation and action as representations of the wings on a bird. In order for the bird to fly, both wings must work together. When one wing flaps, the other wing flips as well. The two wings work together in order to keep the bird moving.

To put this into context, rather than devoting your energy to motivating yourself to learn a new language, just dive in and get started! The motivation will eventually catch up, but only after you take those first few steps.

Here are some ideas to get you started right now:

- Pick a daily phrase from #1 and say it 10 times today.

- Find a popular song in your desired language on FluentU or YouTube and listen to it 5 times in a row.
- Sign up for polyglot Olly Richard's <u>Language Learning Foundations</u> video course, which is designed to help you get set up and started with the ins and outs of learning a new language.
- You may also be interested in his <u>Grammar Hero</u> or <u>Conversations</u> courses, which are designed to help you set up workable, step-by-step systems for learning your target language.
- Pick up your phone and change the device language.

And there you go! These ideas for how to learn a language by yourself may sound crazy at first glance, but sometimes crazy can be exactly what we need to move forward.

CHAPTER THREE

PRACTICING ON YOUR OWN

It is very important to regularly practice what you have learned even if it is just talking out loud to yourself. To really succeed in learning a new language (become fluent), it is essential to practice with a native speaker, but until you have found someone to practice with, here are some ways to practice by yourself.

Think in the new language

One of the main things about learning to speak a language is that you always have to learn to think in the language.

If you're always thinking in English when you speak another language, you need to translate everything in your head while you speak. That's not easy and takes time.

It doesn't matter how fluent you are in a new language; it's always hard to switch between two languages in your mind.

That's why you need to start thinking in the new language as well as speaking it. You can do this during your daily life.

If you discover a new word, reach for your chosen language's monolingual dictionary rather than the bilingual version. (Don't have dictionaries?—Buy some. You will need them; they can be your best friends while learning a new language.)

Think out Loud

Now that you're already thinking in your new language—why don't you think out loud?

Talking to yourself whenever you're on your own is a great way to improve your language-speaking skills.

When you're reading books try doing it out loud, too.

The problem with speaking on your own is when you make mistakes. There's nobody there to correct you.

However, it's helpful to improve your ability to speak out loud, even if you make the occasional error.

Talk to the Mirror

Stand in front of a mirror and talk in your new language.

You could pick a topic to talk about and time yourself.

Can you talk about soccer for two minutes? Can you explain what happened in the news today for three minutes?

While you're talking, you need to watch the movements of your mouth and body.

Don't allow yourself to stop. If you can't remember the particular word, then you need to express the same thing with different words.

After a couple of minutes, it's time to look up any words you didn't know. This will allow you to discover which words and topics you need to work to improve.

Fluency over Grammar

The most important thing when speaking isn't grammar; it's fluency.

You don't want to be stopping and starting all the time. You need to be able to have free-flowing conversations with native speakers.

Don't allow yourself to stop and stumble over phrases. A minor error here and there doesn't matter.

You need to make yourself understood rather than focus on everything being perfect.

24 Failproof Tips for Learning a Language by Yourself

(https://www.onmycanvas.com/how-to-learn-a-language-by-yourself/)

CHAPTER FOUR

SHORT STEPS FOR LEARNING

Listen and repeat over and over

Check out foreign-language TV shows or movies to improve your language skills.

Listen carefully and, then pause and repeat. You can attempt to replicate the accent of the person on the screen.

If you need some help to understand the meaning, turn on subtitles for extra help. If you come across a word you don't recognize, you can look it up in your dictionary.

5 Smart Ways to Learn a Language by Watching TV and Films

Learn some songs

If you want a really fun way to learn a language, you can learn the lyrics to your favorite songs in the new language.

You can start with children's song and work yourself up to the classics.

9 Tips to Learn a Language Through Songs

Learn phrases and common sayings
Instead of concentrating on learning new words—why not try to learn phrases and common sayings?

You can boost your vocabulary and learn how to arrange the words in a sentence like a native speaker.

You need to look out for how native speakers express stuff. You can learn a lot from listening to others.

16 Must-Know words and Phrases for any Language

Imagine different scenarios

Sometimes, you can imagine different scenarios in which you have to talk about different kinds of things.

For example, you can pretend to be in an interview for a job in the country speaking your target language.

You can answer questions such as: "What are your biggest weaknesses?" and "Why do you want to work for us?"

When you have already prepared for such circumstances, you'll know what to say when the time comes.

6 Tips for Acing a Job Interview in a Foreign Language

Change the language on your devices

Consider changing your phone, computer, tablet, Facebook page, and anything else with a language option to your target language. This is an easy way to practice a new language since you'll see more of the vocabulary on a daily basis.

For example, every time you look at your phone, you'll see the date in the target language, reinforcing the days of the week and months of the year. Facebook will ask you if you would like to "add a friend", teaching you the verb that means "to add" in your new language.

Seeing a few of the same words over and over again will help the language feel more natural to you, and you'll find it becomes easier to incorporate them into everyday life with very little effort involved!

How to Change the Language on your Android Phone

How to Change the Language on your iPhone, iPad or iPod

3 Ways to Change the Language on a Cell Phone

10 Genius Ways to Use your Smartphone to Learn a Language

Research in your target language

How many times a day do you Google something that you're curious about? If you use Wikipedia a few times a week, go for the target language version of the website first. Next time you need information about your favorite celebrity, look at their page in the target language and see how much you can understand before switching the language to English!

How to Change the Language in Wikipedia

How to Change the Language in Google Chrome

Pick up a Foreign Newspaper

You can read foreign newspapers online. There are plenty of choices to suit your taste. You can also download apps and read the news on your phone. You can read the articles out loud to practice pronunciation in addition to reading skills. This is also a great way to stay informed about what is happening in the country you are interested in and the world in general, and helps if you get in a conversation in your target language.

Global List of Online Newspapers

Play games in your target language

Once your phone is in your target language, many of your games will appear in that language, too. Trivia games force you to be quick on your feet as you practice, as many of them are timed. If that isn't for you, WordBrain offers an interesting vocabulary challenge in different languages.

9 Great Games for Learning Languages

Watch TV Shows and You Tube videos

Don't knock foreign soap operas until you try them! If you follow any British soaps, you will enjoy them. Netflix, Hulu, Amazon and Apple now offer shows and movies in many other different languages, some of which include English subtitles so you can check how much you understand. You can also watch your favorite movies with subtitles.

Don't have Netflix, Hulu, Amazon or Apple? Try watching on YouTube or downloading straight from the Net. You can also check out free lessons in your target language on YouTube in your spare time. This is a good way to judge the stage your learning has reached. If you are a beginner, look for lessons that teach you how to say the letters and sounds of the TL (target language) alphabet. It will help with your pronunciation.

10 Ways to Use YouTube as a Language Learning Tool

Get TL (target language) music for your daily commute

Why not practice your TL during your commute? Singing along to songs will help your pronunciation and help you begin to think in your TL (not a good idea if you use public transportation unless, of course, you have a superb singing voice). Try to learn the lyrics.

You can get music in any genre on YouTube, just like in English.

Top 50 Non-English songs on YouTube

Listen to podcasts in your TL

While you're sitting at your desk, driving in your car on your way to work, or cooking dinner at home, put on a podcast in your TL. It could be one aimed at teaching in your TL or a podcast on another topic that interests you.

Complete Guide to Foreign Language Podcasts

CHAPTER FIVE

WHY SPEAKING BEATS GRAMMAR EVERY TIME

A lot of people try to learn a language by "studying." They try really hard to memorize grammar rules and vocabulary in the hope that one day, all the pieces will come together and they'll magically start speaking the language.

Sorry, but languages don't work that way.

Trying to speak a language by doing grammar exercises is like trying to make bread by reading cookbooks. Sure, you'll pick up some tips, but you'll never learn how to bake unless you're willing to get your hands dirty.

Languages are a learn-by-doing kind of a deal. The best way to learn to speak, understand, read, and write a language is by practicing speaking, listening, reading, and writing. That doesn't mean you should never study grammar or vocabulary. It helps to get an idea of how the language works. But if you dedicate a disproportionate amount of time to that stuff, it'll clutter your learning experience and hold you back from actually speaking the language.

You'll learn much faster by using the language.

Most learning methods only teach you the "stuff" of the target language, like the grammar, vocabulary, listening, reading, etc. Very few of them actually teach you how to speak the TL.

Let's compare methods.

Methods that only teach you the "stuff" of the target language:

- Apps
- Audio courses
- Group classes
- Radio/podcasts
- Reading
- Software
- Textbooks
- TV/movies

Methods that teach you to speak:

- Practicing with people you know
- Meetups
- Language exchanges
- Lessons with a teacher online or in the real world

Many language experts, like Benny Lewis, have said that studying will never help you speak a language.

The best way to learn any language involves more than just studying.

Let's say you are learning to drive for the first time. Your parents drop you off at the driving school for your theory class.

You spend many hours learning about traffic lights, left turns, parallel parking, and the dreaded roundabout. Your brain is filled with everything you'll ever need to know about driving a car.

Does this mean you can drive now?

No!

There's a reason why they don't give you your license right after you pass the theory test. It's because studying theory doesn't actually teach you how to drive.

You need to be behind the wheel, you need to get a "feel" for it with all of your senses, and you need to get used to making snap decisions.

Languages work in the same way.

To learn a language properly, you have to speak it.

Speaking: The one thing that makes everything else easier

You might be asking, "How am I supposed to speak if I don't learn vocabulary and grammar first?"
While it's true that a small foundation of vocabulary and grammar is necessary, the problem is that most beginners greatly overestimate how much they really need.

People spend thousands of dollars on courses and many months of self-study and still don't feel like they're "ready" to speak. Speaking is something that they'll put off again and again.

Scientists from the NTL Institute (https://www.ntl.org/) discovered through their research that people remember:

90% of what they learn when they use it immediately.

50% of what they learn when engaged in a group discussion.

20% of what they learn from audio-visual sources.

10% of what they learn when they've learned from reading.

5% of what they learn from lectures.

This means that the best way to learn a language is to start speaking from the beginning and try to use every new word and grammar concept in real conversations.

Speaking is the one skill that connects all the different elements of language learning. When you are speaking, you are actually improving every other aspect of the language simultaneously.

Speaking improves:

- Pronunciation
- Reading
- Writing
- Vocabulary
- Grammar
- Listening

Here's a breakdown of how speaking can improve your other language skills:

Vocabulary

Have you ever studied a word in a foreign language but then totally drawn a blank when you tried to use it in a conversation? Well, you will. Sorry.

This happens all the time because, although you can recognize the word when you see it or hear it, you can't naturally recall the word when you want to.

Grammar

Let's say your friend asks you what you did yesterday, and you want to respond in Spanish:

> What is "To walk" in Spanish?

"caminar"

Ok, time to use past tense, but should I use preterit or imperfect?
Preterit because you're talking about a single point in time.

What is the conjugation for "caminar" for the first person?
"caminé"

Your answer: "Ayer, caminé por la playa."

You may have studied all the grammar, but you would probably spend a good ten seconds thinking about this if you're not used to using grammar in conversations.

Speaking is the only thing that trains your brain and speeds up this thought process until you can respond in 1/10th of a second.

Listening

For many beginners, understanding native speakers is the number one challenge when learning a new language.

When you are having a conversation with someone, you are speaking and training your ears at the same time. You are listening "actively," which means you are listening with the intent to respond. This forces you into a higher state of concentration, as opposed to "passively" listening to the radio, for example, where you are simply taking in information.

Listening and speaking really go hand in hand.

Pronunciation

The first part of pronunciation is to understand how to correctly produce the sounds, which can be tricky, once you can do it right, the next part is about getting enough reps and saying the words out loud again and again.

Maybe at first, the words will make your tongue and lips feel strange, but over time, they will become part of your muscle memory until eventually it feels completely natural to say them.

<u>The ten best ways to improve pronunciation in a foreign language</u>

Textbooks

If you're totally new to language learning, you may be wondering how you can start using a language you don't know yet. If you're learning completely from scratch, a good textbook can help you pick up the basics. But avoid ones that teach lots of grammar rules without showing you how to use them in real life. The best textbooks are the ones that give you lots of example conversations and introduce grammar in bite-size pieces.

5 Tips for Selecting the Best Foreign Language Textbooks

As soon as you can, aim to get lots of exposure to the new language being used in a real way. If you're a lower-level learner, you can start by reading books that have been simplified for your level (called graded readers). Look for ones accompanied by audio so you can work on your listening at the same time.

Foreign language graded readers
https://readers.teachyourself.com/

Bullet Journals

If you can, keep a diary or journal of your experience with different methods of learning. Bullet journals are great for this. Never heard of them? They are basically a sort of a cross between a diary and a to-do list. Keeping one will help you see what works for you and what doesn't, and also to chart your progress. You can buy readymade ones to suit you or design your own. You can use it for motivation when you feel like you are getting nowhere, as you will see at a glance all the progress you have made. Believe me, you will be surprised at how far you have come and sometimes you just need a little reminder to give you that motivational push. You will also be able to see what areas you need to improve in and the types of things you are best at. When you are feeling low, go back to the stuff you are best at.

The best bullet journals - all you need to know

Learning like a child

Consider how a child has learned to speak a language. Presumably, unless it was a precocious genius, it did not start off by reading a primer in grammar. Children start off by observing and identifying. Naming and pronunciation comes from hearing the description of the object from others, usually adults, or other kids fluent in the language.

How children learn

CHAPTER SIX

MOTIVATION AND THE COMPLETE BEGINNER

If you are a complete beginner, you should pay just as much attention to how you learn as what you learn.

- Motivation: Defining your overarching goal
- Step by Step: Setting achievable short-term goals
- Getting There: Efficient learning resources for beginners
- Fun: Having fun as you learn
- Ongoing Motivation: Staying motivated as you learn

Definition of Motivation: a reason or reasons for acting or behaving in a particular way.

Motivation is critical for learning a language. Lack of motivation is one of the main reasons people fail to achieve their goal of speaking a new language and give up before they really get started. Good, motivating reasons for learning your TL (target language) include:

- "I want to understand people at TL events."
- "I want to flirt with that cute person at work in their language."
- "I want to read books in the original."
- "I want to understand people at my local TL delicatessen."
- "I want to enjoy TL soap operas or TV series.."
- "I need the TL for work so that I can communicate with clients."
- "I want to be able to make myself understood when I'm on holiday in...."

These are all great reasons for learning a foreign language because they include personal, compelling motivations that'll keep you coming back when the going gets rough.

They also guide you to **specific, achievable goals** for study, like focusing on reading or on the vocabulary used in conversations on the dance floor.

Here are a few bad—but rather common—reasons for learning a foreign language:

- "I want to tell people I speak xxx"
- "I want to have the TL on my CV."
- "I want to look smart."

Why are these bad?:

These are very likely not going to be truly motivating reasons when you can't seem to find time to open that workbook. They also don't give you any concrete desire to pay careful attention to, for example, a new tense that you've come across and how it might allow you to express yourself better.

If looking smart is your honest reason for wanting to learn a language, perhaps you could just lie and say you speak something like Quechua, which few people are going to be able to call you out on. (If you are interested, Quechua was the ancient language of the Incas and is still spoken in remote parts of South America).

It is rarely possible to learn a language without a genuine motivation for some sort of authentic communication. That does not mean it should be painful or boring.

When you are interested in something and having fun you do not have to consciously **TRY**, and strangely, this is when you perform at your best. You are in the zone, as they say.

Step by Step: Setting achievable, short-term goals.

As in life, once you are clear about your overall motivation(s), these should then be translated into achievable, short-term goals.

You're not going to immediately get every joke passed around the pub or the party and be able to respond in kind, but you should be able to more quickly arrive at goals like:

- "I'm going to place my favorite restaurant order in my TL."
- "I'm going to memorize and use three words of TL slang."

I cannot stress enough the importance of correct pronunciation, as this will form the basis of your learning experience. There are a lot of free online pronunciation guides, make the most of them. It is also a good idea, if you have the equipment to record yourself and compare it to the native speaker.

Talk when you read or write in the TL. Writing itself is an important part of language learning so read out loud (paying careful attention to pronunciation) and write in the TL as much as you can. Just like when you took notes at school, writing serves to reinforce your learning.

- Watch movies with subtitles. Imitate some of the characters if you want.
- Listen to music in your TL, learn the lyrics of your favorite songs, and sing along with them.
- Join a local TL group. You'd be surprised how many there are and how helpful they can be for new language learners. This will give you a chance to practice your TL with a native speaker in a friendly and helpful environment.

CHAPTER SEVEN

FLUENCY

What is fluency? Every person has a different answer to that question. The term is imprecise, and it means a little less every time someone writes another book, article, or spam email with a title like "U can B fluent in 7 days!"

A lot of people are under the impression that to be fluent in another language means to speak it as well as, or almost as well as, your native language. These people define fluency as knowing a language perfectly—lexically, grammatically and even phonetically. If that is the case, then I very much doubt that there are that many fluent English speakers out there. By that, I mean that they know every aspect of English grammar and know every word in the English language.

I prefer to define it as "being able to speak and write quickly or easily in a given language." It comes from the Latin word fluentum, meaning "to flow."

There is also a difference between translating and interpreting, though they are often confused. The easiest way to remember the difference is that translating deals with the written word while interpreting deals with the spoken word. I suppose, to be pedantic, one should be fluent in both forms, but for most people, when they think of fluency, they mean the spoken word. Nobody has ever asked me to write them something in Spanish, for instance, but I am quite often asked to say something in Spanish, as though this somehow proves my fluency—which is a bit weird when you think about it as it is only people who have no knowledge of Spanish whatsoever who ask me that and I could say any old nonsense and they would believe it was Spanish.

The next question most people ask is: how long does it take to be fluent? It is different for every person. But let's use an example to make a baseline calculation. To estimate the time you'll need, you need to consider your fluency goals, the language(s) you already know, the language you're learning, and your daily time constraints.

One language is not any more difficult to learn than another; it just depends on how difficult it is for you to learn. For example, Japanese may be difficult to learn for many English speakers for the same reason that English is difficult for many Japanese speakers; there are very few words and grammar concepts that overlap, plus an entirely different alphabet. In contrast, an English speaker learning French has much less work to do. English vocabulary is 28% French and 28% Latin, so as soon as an English speaker learns French pronunciation, they already know thousands of words. If you want to check the approximate difficulty of learning a new language for an English speaker, you can check with the US Foreign Service Institute, which grades them by "class hours needed to learn."

FSI research indicates that it takes 480 hours to reach basic fluency in group 1 languages, and 720 hours for group 2-4 languages. If we are able to put in 10 hours a day to learn a language, then basic fluency in the easy languages should take 48 days, and for difficult languages 72 days.

But here's the good news:

You can cut down the time it takes to learn a language with these 6 tricks:

1. Make your language study sessions shorter but more frequent

It's tempting to think that because learning a language takes hundreds or thousands of hours, it's a good idea to just sit down for ten hours straight and knock off a real chunk of the time you're going to have to put in.

Not so fast though!

If you want to cut down how much time you have to spend learning a language, the trick isn't just to study as much as possible, but to **divide up your work** into shorter, more frequent study sessions.

There are two obvious ways this method speeds up your language learning:

- By doing frequent study sessions, you're keeping the language fresh in your mind. If you take extended breaks from language learning, you'll lose ground and end up having to spend more time getting back to where you were.
- By avoiding unnecessarily long and drawn-out study sessions, you're keeping your mind sharp and firing on all cylinders (or at least more cylinders), which makes your learning more efficient and therefore faster.

However, the main benefit of short but frequent language learning sessions is that something fundamentally different is happening in your brain when you study something, go do something else, then come back and study it some more (as opposed to just studying it for longer with no break in the middle).

Specifically, while you're off doing non-language-related things, your brain is still consolidating what you've learned. By going back and continuing your studying in the relatively near future, **you're reinforcing what you've learned** and building on the knowledge your brain has consolidated. But wait too long, and this knowledge starts to dissolve away.

For example, say you have a list of vocab words you want to learn. Suppose you can either (a) study the list twice, then wait two days, then study it twice again, or (b) you can study it once a day for four days.

In both cases, you're doing the same amount of studying, but the latter approach is probably going to be more successful. Why? Because by doing shorter, more frequent study sessions, you're getting a better balance of consolidation and reinforcement.

To apply a little bit of pressure to a familiar analogy: Language learning is a war, not a battle, and to win the war you have to make the battles shorter and more frequent.

In practice, it can take a little creativity to make the "short and frequent study sessions" approach work. Some techniques you can use to stick to this kind of schedule are:

- Give each study session a limited, concrete goal, especially on days when you're pressed for time. For example: "I'm going to translate this excerpt," "I'm going to review my vocab words," or "I'm going to listen to this podcast episode," etc.
- On days when it seems like you really aren't going to be able to fit in any language learning, you have three options: (1) make a list of everything you're doing that day and see if you can shave even five to ten minutes off of any of your other activities, (2) do five to ten minutes of studying first thing in the morning or (3) do five to ten minutes of studying right before you go to bed.
- Review is less time-consuming than learning entirely new material, and it's better to do lots

of lightning quick review sessions than nothing at all if you're going through an especially busy time.
- One of the basic illusions of time management is that if you plan out how you're using your time in advance, it seems like you actually have more time. Try to schedule as many of your study sessions in advance as possible.

2. Use repetition strategically

Unless you have a photographic memory, language learning isn't going to happen without a healthy dose of repetition. You'll often have to review material multiple times before you get it to stick.

However, it's not just a question of how much repetition you do. The quickest path to learning a new vocab word isn't necessarily just to repeat that word as much as possible.

The reason for this is that timing is everything. When you repeat things also matters.

Specifically, psychology researchers have long known that it's easier to learn something when you repeat it at increasing rather than even intervals. For example, if you're learning a vocab word, you'll learn it more quickly by looking it up, then reviewing it a few seconds later, then a few minutes later, then a few hours later, then a few days later and so on, rather than just reviewing it every 24 hours.

This effect is called spaced repetition, and it's something a lot of language learning software takes advantage of.

But you can also use it yourself to optimize your study habits. The idea is simple: When you learn something, review it multiple times with increasing intervals between your review sessions. You can even draw up a basic schedule the first time you learn it to keep track of when you want to do your repetitions.

Coming up with an optimal schedule is part art and part science, so it'll take some experimentation, but a good rule of thumb to use as a starting place is that ideally you'll have at least one review session within a matter of minutes, at least one review session within a matter of hours, at least one within a matter of days and at least one within a matter of weeks.

For more challenging material, it's often especially helpful to add extra sessions at the "days" level since it's generally not helpful to move on to "weeks" until you have it down pretty well.

This technique will really cut down your language learning time for a couple of reasons. First, because it's a general rule for how learning happens best, you can apply it to any material you're studying.

And second, the amount of repetition involved is the main reason it takes so long to learn a language, so anything you can do to make sure you have to repeat things as few times as possible will go a long way towards speeding up the process.

3. Make the language relevant to your life

Here's a pretty simple truth: We remember things that matter to us and we forget things that don't.

Language is no exception. And when we treat language as nothing more than a bunch of words on a piece of paper, we make it something that doesn't matter.

If you want to learn a language quickly and efficiently, finding ways to make the language relevant to your life should be a top priority. The problem with trying to learn a language that's not relevant to your life is that you'll find yourself forgetting what you've been learning more often, and the problem with forgetting things is that it takes a lot of time—because then you have to relearn them!

So how can you make a foreign language relevant to your life?

The best way is to take a two-pronged approach.

In the long term, you need to be clear about your goals, about why you're learning the language. Maybe you're going to a country where they speak the language, maybe you're drawn to a culture or literature associated with the language, maybe you know people who speak the language. Whatever it is, there should be some reason becoming fluent in the language is actually relevant to your life.

In the short term, you need to use the language, not just study it. Finding activities you enjoy that involve the language (reading books, watching movies, cooking, etc.) is important because things you enjoy are by definition relevant to your life! Getting someone to talk to can also do wonders for picking up your learning pace.

When you have a powerful long-term motivation for learning a language and when you have things you're using the language for in the short term, all the studying you're doing really matters. Whether or not you remember what you're learning suddenly has real consequences in terms of your ability to engage in these short-term activities and meet these long-term goals.

If you don't yet know how your target language connects directly to the things you care about, take some of the time you've set aside for language learning and brainstorm as many ways as possible to complete each of the following statements:

- I want to learn this language so that I can...
- Once I'm fluent in this language, I will be able to..
- If I don't succeed in learning this language, I won't be able to...

Then take as many of the things you wrote down and start doing them as soon as possible—especially before you feel "ready."

Making the language personally relevant is the most direct way of calling up your brain and saying "hey, brain, this stuff is important to me, so you'd better remember it!" And the more you remember, the less you have to repeat, the faster you learn.

4. Speak the language like your life depends on it

There's a difference between studying a language and learning a language.

Studying a language implies memorizing new vocab, getting to know new grammatical constructions, maybe following some kind of course–all that stuff. Studying a language is good.

Learning a language implies actually internalizing it and getting to the point where you can use it to communicate. Studying is important, but learning is the goal.

Now, studying is an important part of learning a language, but **it's not enough to get you all the way**. To really learn a language, you have to use it. Studying gives you the raw materials you need to learn a language, but to make those materials into something meaningful and memorable, you have to use them to put together sentences and convey ideas.

Therefore, to learn a language faster, you need to speak the language any and every chance you get. When you use what you've learned by speaking the language, it becomes a part of you and you'll ultimately have to spend much less time rehashing it and trying to get it to stick.

A great way to create opportunities to speak the language is by finding people to talk to, either online, offline or both.

But you shouldn't limit yourself to talking to other people. Talk to yourself. After all, you're around yourself 24/7, so you're your own most accessible conversation partner. Some ways of learning by talking to yourself are:

- **Have conversations with yourself out loud**. You can either have conversations with yourself about topics you'd normally think about anyway, or you can create dialogues between fictional characters. Try to keep the flow of things going like you would in a normal conversation.
- **Keep a journal**. Write regular entries about your life, your thoughts or any topic you're interested in. This is also a good way of making the language more personally relevant.
- **Record yourself speaking.** Once you've got the recording, listen to it and try repeating back sentences to correct pronunciation, grammar, etc. as necessary. Record yourself

both speaking spontaneously and using a prepared text (which will allow you to do multiple "takes"). Or you can combine these two approaches by doing the first take spontaneously, then listening back and creating a written transcript of what you said, then reading the transcript back and recording yourself.
- **Narrate an inner monologue in your new language.** Push yourself to use a rich vocabulary and varied grammatical constructions

Anything that gets you speaking the language cuts down how much time it's going to take you to reach fluency. Speak the language like your life depends on it, and you'll find studying translates into learning much more quickly, reducing the amount of time you have to spend studying overall.

5. Use these three apps to make language learning part of your daily life

One of the easier parts of language learning is how flexible the process is. You can study whenever you want for however long you want and still make progress–even very short study sessions can be very helpful.

With this in mind, one of the best things you can do to speed up your language learning is to take advantage of idle moments you have throughout the day to sneak in just a little language learning here and there.

Interspersing little slices of language learning throughout your daily life will shave time off your core study sessions, and it'll also keep the language fresh in your mind and thus make your learning more efficient. After all, the idea of doing micro-study sessions at intervals over the course of your day is just an extreme version of doing shorter, more frequent study sessions.

If you own a smartphone, an incredibly simple way to make language learning part of your daily life is by installing these three apps (and using them!):

- **Any dictionary app**. Make a habit of asking yourself "I wonder how you say ~ in [target language]," and then looking up the word you're curious about in your dictionary app. Two good options are Google Translate and iTranslate, though a dictionary specifically for your target language will probably be more accurate (i.e. Spansh, German, French, Chinese, Japanese, Italian, Korean, Russian).
- **Any flashcard app**. There's never a dull moment when you have flashcards! Okay, that might be a stretch, but with one of these flashcard apps you can go into language learning mode at the drop of a dime.
- **FluentU.** FluentU lets you learn a language using real-world videos, and the app provides a sort of multimedia smartphone immersion experience. Besides helping you work a little language studying into your daily schedule, the FluentU app has the added benefit of

giving you an excuse to take a minute and chill out watching cool videos.

6. Create a sustainable language learning plan that works

Learning efficiently isn't something that's just going to happen by itself. If you want to learn quickly, you have to plan to learn quickly.

Part of this is coming up with a language learning road map that includes time-saving language learning strategies–working language learning into your day with smartphone apps, using repetition to your advantage, speaking the language as much as possible, engaging in activities that make the language relevant to your life and doing short but frequent study sessions.

However, you also need to **make sure your language learning plan is sustainable**. When you're looking to learn a language as fast as possible, it can be tempting to try to just power through a superhuman amount of material in record time.

The problem is, if you burn yourself out by trying to do too much at once, your motivation will fizzle and your language learning will end up taking more time in the end.

This is a case where slow and steady wins the race. Well, okay, maybe not slow. But steady is definitely something to strive for.

When designing your language learning plan, you want to make sure you have a specific strategy for how you're going to improve in each of the following areas: vocabulary, grammar, listening, speaking, writing and reading.

You also want to make sure a good chunk of your activities will improve your general fluency by giving you an opportunity to integrate everything you're learning. For example, having a weekly conversation with a language exchange partner is both a chance to improve your speaking and an exercise that you can use to improve general fluency.

Once you set your language learning plan in motion, keep tabs on whether it's working in a sustainable way. In particular, if you're making much more progress in some areas than others, revise your plan to spend more time on or to change your methods for the areas you're falling behind in.

And if you find yourself consistently failing to meet your goals and stay on pace with your schedule, that's a red flag that your plan isn't sustainable and that you should go back and make it less dense.

So make sure you're starting with an approach that works both in the sense that you're using effective learning techniques and in the sense that you'll be able to keep up your energy and commitment from beginning to end.

If you can do that, and if you use these tricks to optimize your language learning, you'll probably be surprised by how fast those five hundred hours fly by. Instead of asking "Shouldn't I be fluent by now?" you'll find yourself wondering "How did I learn an entire language already?"

CHAPTER EIGHT

LEARNING LIKE A CHILD

Why is it that when we look back to our childhood, it seems that we effortlessly learned the things we truly wanted to?

There are a number of factors that we can look at individually.

- To start with, there seems to be a misinformed idea that as young adults, we have less on our minds and that this makes learning something like another language that much easier.

Mindfulness. Before you turn away in disgust and throw this book to the other side of the room shouting, "I knew it! He was a hippy all along. Now he is going to get me to cross my legs and hum OM," I am not going to ask you to do any of those things. If that is your thing, though, please feel free to do it, although I will remain dubious as to whether it will help you master another language.

I know mindfulness is a bit of a buzzword nowadays. A lot of people have heard about it but are confused about what it really means. This is not a book about mindfulness, so I am just going to go over the basics. It means focusing your awareness on the present moment and noticing your physical and emotional sensations without judgment as you are doing whatever you happen to be doing.

The benefits of mindfulness are plentiful. It increases concentration, improves self-acceptance and self-esteem, strengthens resilience, and decreases stress. In a world where we are continually subject to stress mindfulness can provide an oasis of calm.

Mindfulness (being mindful of what you do), can also help you to learn a language much more easily because a part of mindfulness involves unconscious concentration. To achieve unconscious concentration as an adult we have to practice it, unfortunately, as it is a skill many of us have lost. It is not as difficult as it sounds, and in fact, it is quite fun. Just take time out, if you get a chance, and watch some young children at play.

Look at how hard children concentrate in whatever game they are playing. They aren't making a conscious effort to concentrate; they are concentrating naturally, thoroughly immersed in the game. This is mindfulness in its most natural form, and this is what thousands of people pay hundreds of bucks every year to achieve once again.

Now, see what happens if you get one of the poor kids to stop playing and ask them to do a mundane and pre-set task like taking out the trash. Watch the child's attitude change: she's now, not just annoyed and resentful that she has been taken away from her game, but the concentration that was there when she was playing has gone. You could say her mind's not on the job, and you would be quite right. The mindfulness has gone, but it will return almost instantaneously when she resumes playing and having fun.

Games, puzzles, and challenges are all fun to us when we are young and we devote all our mind's energy to them wholeheartedly, and that is what we will try to recapture as we learn our target language (TL).

When you are actively concentrating on learning the TL, it is a good idea to turn off all distractions except the method you are using to learn. By this, I mean all the gadgets we are surrounded by, such as: the telephone, radio, Facebook, Twitter, Instagram—you get the picture.

Multitasking is one of those words that is bandied about a lot nowadays—the ability to perform lots of tasks at the same time. But in this particular case, multitasking is a bad thing, a very bad thing. It has been proven that it isn't actually healthy for us and we are more efficient when we focus on just one thing at a time.

Take some deep breaths and focus all your attention on your breath. You will find your mind wandering and thoughts will distract you, but don't try to think them through or control them. Bring your attention back to your breath. It takes practice, and like learning your TL, if you do it every day, you will get better at it. Also, learning to breathe better will bring more oxygen to your brain.

Before you start any learning, take a few moments to breathe and relax. If you want, do some light stretching. This allows for better blood flow before studying. Better blood flow means more oxygen to the brain—need I say more?

When it comes to studying, do the same as you did with your thoughts: if you make a mistake, do not judge yourself. Instead, acknowledge it and move on. Be kind to yourself at all times. You are doing an awesome thing—be proud of it. Remember that old saying: you learn through your mistakes. It is fine to make mistakes; just remember to learn from them and not get annoyed with yourself.

Just like with being mindful, be aware of the progress you are making with your language learning, but also be patient and do not judge yourself or compare yourself with others.

If you feel like it, smile a bit (I don't mean grin like a madman) as studies have shown that smiling brings authentic feelings of well-being and reduces stress levels.

You will find your mind wandering. Everybody's mind wanders. This is fine and completely normal. Just sit back and look at the thought. Follow it but do not take part. Be an observer, as it were. You can label it if that makes it easier to dismiss, for example, "worrying," "planning," "judging," etc. It is up to you to either act upon that and become distracted or let it go and focus on the task at hand—learning your target language.

CHAPTER NINE

SHORT STEPS TO SPEAKING A FOREIGN LANGUAGE (CONCLUSIONS)

Conversation, conversation, conversation

If there's a "secret" or "hack" to learning a new language, it's this: hours and hours of awkward and strenuous conversation with people better than you in that language. An hour of conversation (with corrections and a dictionary for reference) is as good as five hours in a classroom and 10 hours with a language course by yourself.

There are a few reasons for this. The first is motivation. I don't care how cool your study guide is, you're going to be far more invested and motivated to communicate with a live person in front of you than a book or audio program on your computer.

The second reason is that language is something that needs to be processed, not memorized. Staring and memorizing a word in a book or with flashcards 100 times simply does not stick the same way as being forced to use a word in conversation a mere two or three times.

The reason is that our minds place more priority on memories which involve actual human and social experiences, memories which have emotions tied to them.

So, for instance, if I look up the verb for "to complain" and use it in a sentence with a new friend, chances are I'm always going to associate that word with that specific interaction and conversation I was having with her. Whereas I can blow by that same word 20 times with flashcards, and even though I may get it right, I haven't actually practiced implementing it. It means nothing to me, so it is less likely to stick with me.

Nobody ever wanted to learn a new language so they can stay in their house and watch soap operas in that language all day.

So, if the goal is to speak a foreign language, then why do the majority of beginners start learning using methods that don't actually force them to speak?

This is the single biggest mistake that most people make when learning Spanish, German, French or any other language.

Most learning methods only teach you the "stuff" of a foreign language, like the grammar, vocabulary, listening, reading, etc. Very few of them actually teach you how to speak the language.

Methods that only teach you the "stuff" of a foreign language:

- Apps
- Audio courses
- Group classes
- Radio/podcasts
- Reading
- Software
- Textbooks
- TV/movies

Methods that teach you to speak a foreign language:

- Practicing with people you know
- Meetups
- Language exchanges
- Lessons with a TL teacher online or in the real world

Many language experts, like Benny Lewis, have said that studying will never help you speak a language. The best way to learn any foreign language involves more than just studying.

Let's say you are learning to drive for the first time. Your parents drop you off at the driving school for your theory class.

You spend many hours learning about traffic lights, left turns, parallel parking, and the dreaded roundabout.

Your brain is filled with everything you'll ever need to know about driving a car.

Does this mean you can drive now?
No!

There's a reason why they don't give you your license right after you pass the theory test. It's because studying theory doesn't actually teach you how to drive.

You need to be behind the wheel, you need to get a "feel" for it with all of your senses, and you need to get used to making snap decisions.

Languages work in the same way.

To learn a language properly, you have to speak it.

Speaking: The one thing that makes everything else easier

You might be asking, "How am I supposed to speak if I don't learn vocabulary and grammar first?"

While it's true that a small foundation of vocabulary and grammar is necessary, the problem is that most beginners greatly overestimate how much they really need.

People spend thousands of dollars on courses and many months of self-study and still don't feel like

they're "ready" to speak in their TL. Speaking is something that they'll put off again and again.
Scientists from the NTL Institute discovered through their research that people remember:

90% of what they learn when they use it immediately.

50% of what they learn when engaged in a group discussion.

20% of what they learn from audio-visual sources.

10% of what they learn when they've learned from reading.

5% of what they learn from lectures.

This means that the best way to learn a foreign language is to start speaking from the beginning and try to use every new word and grammar concept in real conversations.

Speaking is the one skill that connects all the different elements of language learning. When you are speaking, you are actually improving every other aspect of the language simultaneously.

Speaking improves:

- Pronunciation
- Reading
- Writing
- Vocabulary

- Grammar
- Listening

Here's a breakdown of how speaking can improve your other language skills:

Vocabulary

Have you ever studied a word in your TL but then totally drawn a blank when you tried to use it in a conversation? Well, you will. Sorry.

This happens all the time because, although you can recognize the word when you see it or hear it, you can't naturally recall the word when you want to.

The only way for new words to truly become part of your vocabulary is to speak them repeatedly, putting them into real sentences that have real meaning. Eventually, the word will become a force of habit so that you can say it without even thinking.

Grammar

Let's say your friend asks you what you did yesterday, and you want to respond in Spanish:

>What is "To walk" in Spanish?
>"caminar"

>Ok, time to use past tense, but should I use preterit or imperfect?
>Preterit because you're talking about a single point in time.

What is the conjugation for "caminar" for the first person?
"caminé"

Your answer: "Ayer, caminé a la playa."

You may have studied all the grammar, but you would probably spend a good ten seconds thinking about this if you're not used to using grammar in conversations.

Speaking is the only thing that trains your brain and speeds up this thought process until you can respond in 1/10th of a second.

Listening

For many beginners, understanding native speakers is the number one challenge when learning Norwegian or any other language.

When you are having a conversation with someone, you are speaking and training your ears at the same time. You are listening "actively," which means you are listening with the intent to respond. This forces you into a higher state of concentration, as opposed to "passively" listening to the radio for example, where you are simply taking in information.

Listening and speaking really go hand in hand.

Pronunciation

The first part of pronunciation is to understand how to correctly produce the sounds, which can be tricky, once you can do it right, the next part is about getting enough reps and saying the words out loud again and again.

Maybe at first, the words will make your tongue and lips feel strange, but over time, they will become part of your muscle memory until eventually it feels completely natural to say them.

Reading and writing

If you can say something in your target language, then you'll have no problem reading and writing it as well.

However, the opposite isn't true. If you focus on reading and writing, it will not enable you to speak better.

Why?

Because, when you're speaking, everything happens in **seconds**, whereas reading and writing happen in **minutes**. Only speaking will train your brain to think fast enough to keep up with conversations.

80/20 your studying

Also called Pareto's principle, the 80/20 rule states that 80% of your results come from just 20% of your efforts.

Vocabulary and grammar

- The 300 most common words make up 65% of spoken dialogue
- The 1,000 most common words make up 88% of spoken dialogue

So, as you can see, you don't NEED to learn every single last word. Start by focusing on the most common words and the words that are personally going to be useful to you based on your interests and goals.

Just like vocabulary, you want to focus on the most common grammar rules and conjugations (ex. present, preterit, future, conditional, etc.). There are lots of advanced grammar rules that aren't used very often in everyday speech, so they are simply less of a priority.

Learning methods

It seems like there are a million ways to learn foreign languages these days, from traditional methods, like textbooks, to endless online resources. This creates a big problem for language learners: a lack of focus. A lot of people try to dabble in as many as five or six different learning methods and end up spreading themselves too thin.

Instead, choose the one or two methods that are most effective (giving you 80% of the results) and ignore the rest. Let's start by outlining some of the methods you could choose for your TL learning.

Popular learning methods

Which methods work, and which ones should you not bother with? Here is a subjective low down.

The reasons why 99% of software and apps won't make you fluent

Take a second and think of all the people you know who learned your target language or any second language.

Did any of them become fluent by learning from an app?

Packed with fancy features, there are hundreds of apps and software out there that claim to be the ultimate, game-changing solution to help you learn a language.

- "Advanced speech recognition system!"
- "Adaptive learning algorithm..."
- "Designed by German scientists."
- "Teaches you a language in just three weeks!"

But do they really work? Is an app really the best way to learn a foreign language?

Or should you file this stuff under the same category as the "Lose 30 pounds in 30 days" diet?

The biggest software and app companies, like Rosetta Stone, Babbel, Busuu, and Duolingo, have all funded their own "independent" studies on the effectiveness of their software. In other words, they all paid the same researcher, who came to the conclusion that every single one of the apps was the best thing since sliced bread.

For example, the study for Babbel concluded:
"...*Users need on average 21 hours of study in a two-month period to cover the requirements for one college semester of the TL.*"

This is no surprise because the fill-in-the-blanks, multiple-choice, one-word-at-a-time approach of software is the same kind of stuff you would find on a foreign language midterm in college.

The problem is that just like software, college and high school foreign language courses are notorious for teaching students a few basics while leaving them completely unable to actually speak.

At the end of the day, software and apps, just like the traditional courses you take in school, are missing a key ingredient: speaking with real people.

The best and fastest way to learn a foreign language is to spend as much time as possible having real conversations. It's the way that languages have been learned for thousands of years, and although technology can help make this more convenient, it cannot be replaced.

Software companies like Rosetta Stone have finally realized this, and in recent years, they've tried to incorporate some sort of speaking element into their product.

The verdict? Their top review on Amazon was one out of five stars.

Ouch! But if software and apps can't really teach you to speak a language, then why are they so popular?

Because they've turned language learning into a game. Every time you get an answer right, there's a little "beep" that tells you that you did a great job, and soon enough, you are showered with badges, achievements, and cute little cartoons that make it feel like you're really getting it. Of course, these things are also used to guilt you into continuing to use their app. If you stop using them, they start sending you pictures of sad cartoon characters telling you they will die because of your lack of commitment. Really? Do they think we've all turned into four-year-olds?

In the real world, playing this game shields you from the difficult parts of learning a language. You can hide in your room, stare at your phone, and avoid the nervousness that comes with speaking a foreign language in front of a native speaker or the awkward moment when you forget what to say.

But the reality is, every beginner who wants to learn a foreign language will have to face these challenges sooner or later.

The 1% of apps that are actually useful

Despite the drawbacks of software and apps, there is one type of app that can have a profound impact on your learning, and we have been here before:

Electronic flashcards (also known as SRS, or "spaced repetition systems").

I know they don't sound very glamorous, and maybe the last time you saw a flashcard was in the hands of that nerdy kid in fifth grade that who nobody wanted to sit with at lunchtime.

But please, bear with me because this can totally change the way you learn a foreign language. Here's how a flashcard system works on an app.

Each flashcard will show you an English word, and you have to try and recall the TL word. If you get it wrong, it will show you the card again in one minute, but if you get it right, it will be a longer interval, like 10 minutes or a few days.

A typical basic flashcard app is Anki. (https://apps.ankiweb.net/).

Flashcard apps work by repeatedly forcing you to recall words that you struggle to remember, and as you get better, the word shows up less and less frequently. As soon as you feel like you're going to forget a new word, the flashcard will pop up and refresh it.

This system helps you form very strong memories and will allow you to manage a database of all the words you've learned, even those you picked up months or years ago.

You can also use flashcards for grammar concepts. For example, if you're having trouble remembering the conjugations for verbs, just make each conjugation a separate flashcard.
By putting all your conjugations in all the different tenses into flashcards, you now have a way to repeatedly drill them into your memory.

The major advantage of flashcards is that all you really need is 10-20 minutes a day. Every single day, we spend a lot of time waiting around, whether it's for public transportation, in line at the supermarket, or for a doctor's appointment. This is all wasted time that you can use to improve your vocabulary. It only takes a few seconds to turn on the flashcard app and review a few words.

If you want to try this out, these are probably the two best apps out there:

Anki (https://apps.ankiweb.net/)
The original, "pure" flashcard app.

Pros:
- Reviewing cards is extremely simple and straightforward.
- Very easy to write your own cards; it can be done on the fly.

- Plenty of customization options and user-written decks to download (although not as many as Memrise).

Cons:
- It can be a bit confusing to set up; you need to be tech-savvy.
- It doesn't provide reminders/motivation to practice daily.

Cost:
- Free for Android, computer.
- US$24.99 for iOS. (At time of writing)

Memrise (https://www.memrise.com)

Flashcard-based app with modern features.

Pros:
- More variety for reviewing cards (fill-in-the-blanks, audio recordings, etc.).
- Offers a little bit of gamification (rewards, reminders) to keep you motivated.
- It has a big library of card decks written by other people and a large community of users.

Cons:
- Writing your own cards (called "Create a Course") is not as easy as Anki and can't be done on mobile.
- The review system works differently from traditional cards.

Cost:
- Free for all platforms (iOS, Android, computer).

Both apps come with standard foreign vocabulary decks as well as those written by other users. However, the real beauty of flashcards is being able to write the decks yourself. There is a big advantage to doing this, which you can see from the following steps:

When using pre-written flashcards

- You see a new word for the first time in your app and then review the word until you remember it.

When making flashcards yourself

- You get exposed to a new world through conversation, your teacher, or something you've seen or heard. You associate the word with a real-life situation.
- You write it into a flashcard, and by doing this, you're already strengthening your memory of that word.
- You review the word until you remember it.

As you can see, while making the cards yourself takes a bit of extra work, you get to control the words you learn and can focus on the ones that are more meaningful to you. Plus, the process of writing the word down acts as an extra round of review.

While it is true that flashcard apps have a bit of a learning curve, they are very easy once you get the hang of them, and you'll notice a huge difference in memorizing vocabulary and grammar.

Intensity of study trumps length of study

What I mean by this is that studying a language four hours a day for two weeks will be more beneficial for you than studying one hour a day for two months. This is one reason why so many people take language classes in school and never remember anything. It's because they only study 3-4 hours per week and often the classes are separated by multiple days.

Language requires a lot of repetition, a lot of reference experiences, and a consistent commitment and investment. It's better to allot a particular period of your life, even if it's only 1-2 weeks, and really go at it 100%, than to half-ass it over the course of months or even years.

Classes are an insufficient use of time and money

All things considered, you get a really poor return for your time and effort in group classes. There are two problems. The first is that the class moves at the pace of its slowest student. The second is that language learning is a fairly personal process—everyone naturally learns some words or topics easier than others, therefore a class is not going to be able to address each student's personal needs as well or in a timely fashion.

For instance, when I took Italian classes I found verb conjugations to be simple because I had already learned Spanish. But an English classmate struggled quite a bit with them. As a result, I spent a lot of my class time waiting around for him to catch up.

I also had a German classmate who had already been exposed to cases, whereas I had no clue what they were. I'm sure he ended up waiting around for me to figure it out as well. The larger the classroom, the less efficient it's going to be. Anyone who had to take a foreign language in school and retained absolutely none of it can tell you this.

Know your motivation

It's silly to even have to say this, but knowing why you're learning a foreign language is key to mastering it. Many people start learning a language with no idea of what they'll use it for. And, sure enough, they fail. You can know all the tips and tricks there are to learning a language, but if you don't know the why behind it all, how it's going to enrich your life, chances are you're going to lose motivation and the learning will fizzle out like an engine sputtering out of gas.

Are you looking to start a new life in a different country? Are you learning a language because you're fascinated by the culture and want to dive in at the deep end? Are you planning a trip to a foreign land and simply wanting to be able to order street food and tell the taxi driver where you're going in the local language? These are all good motivations to learn a language.

And yes, there are bad ones too. If you want to learn Russian simply to impress that cute Russian you met at the bar, if you're thinking of picking up French phrases to impress people and look smart, well, I have bad news for you.

Motivation is a tricky thing. You can will yourself to learn something difficult for a short period of time. But in the long-run, you need to be reaping some practical benefit from your efforts. Without that, you'll eventually burn out.

Set learning goals

Language-learning goals are best if they are short, simple and easily measurable. Many of us embark on studying a language by saying, "I want to be fluent in Japanese in six months!"

The problem is, what is fluency? Fluent in what way? Casual conversation? Reading and writing? Discussing legal issues for your business?

Instead, it's better to set clearly defined goals. Start with something like, "By the end of today, I will know how to greet someone and introduce myself. In two days, I will learn how to ask someone what they do for a living and explain to them what I do. By the end of the week, I will know how to procure food and avoid starvation."

And to get you started, I'll give you the goal of all goals, the milestone that will take you furthest on the path to fluency: "Master the 100 most common words in X weeks/months."

Start with the 100 most common words
Not all vocabulary is created equal. Some give you a better return on investment than others.

Start with the 100 most common words and then make sentences with them over and over again. Learn just enough grammar to be able to do this and do it until you feel pretty comfortable with all of them.

Carry a pocket dictionary when you go abroad

If you don't fancy lugging a physical pocket dictionary around with you it is now super easy to download one onto your phone. Having it on your phone is great, because it takes two seconds to look something up in the middle of conversation. And because you're using it in conversation, you're that much more likely to recall it later. Even something this simple can affect your ability to converse and interact with locals.

Keep practicing in your head

The other use for your dictionary is that you can practice while going about your day and not talking to anyone. Challenge yourself to think in the new language. We all have monologues running in our head, and typically they run in our native tongue. You can continue to practice and construct sentences and fake conversations in your head in a new language. In fact, this sort of visualization leads to much easier conversations when you actually have them.

For instance, you can envision and practice a conversation about a topic you're likely to have before you actually have it. You can begin to think about how you would describe your job and explain why you're in the foreign country in the new language. Inevitably, those questions will come up and you'll be ready to answer them.

You're going to say a lot of stupid things. Accept it...

Learn to shrug off your mistakes because you will make plenty as you learn a new language. Most of these will be funny and you are sure to make a lot of people laugh, which is a sure way of making new friends. If not you're hanging with the wrong crowd.

Figure out pronunciation patterns

All Latin-based languages will have similar pronunciation patterns based on Latin words. For instance, any word that ends in "-tion" in English will almost always end in "-ción" in Spanish and "-ção" in Portuguese. English-speakers are notorious for simply adding "-o" "-e" or "-a" to the end of English words to say Spanish words they don't know. But stereotypes aside, it's surprising how often it's correct. "Destiny" is "destino," "motive" is "motivo," "part" is "parte" and so on. In Russian, case endings always rhyme with one another, so if you are talking about a feminine noun (such as "Zhen-shee-na"), then you know that the adjectives and adverbs will usually rhyme with its ending ("krasee-vaya" as opposed to "krasee-vee").

For a language-learning method that focuses on pronunciation, check out The Mimic Method (https://www.mimicmethod.com/welcome-mark-manson-visitors/)

Use audio and online courses for the first 100 words and basic grammar

After that they should only be used for reference and nothing more. There are a lot of study materials out there (I recommend Benny Lewis' Language Hacking courses, but there are tons). These courses are great for getting you from absolutely no ability in a language to being able to speak basic sentences and phrases within a few days' time. They're also good for teaching the most fundamental vocabulary (words such as: the, I, you, eat, want, thanks, etc.).

There is no shortage of language apps for you to take your pick: Babbel, Memrise, and Duolingo being the most popular ones. Each has its own shortcomings. None is a magic pill that gives you miraculous language abilities. But there is no doubt you can use them to complement your learning. If anything, the crowd-sourced sentences Duolingo uses to teach you grammar and vocabulary will provide great entertainment (and often a peek into what goes on in the minds of the people whose language you're attempting to learn).

But remember, the greatest return on investment in language learning is forcing yourself to speak and communicate with others, and when you're sitting in your bedroom with a book or a software program, you're not being forced to formulate meaning and significance in the new language on the spot. Instead, you're encouraged to parrot and copy concepts and patterns you've observed elsewhere in the materials. These are two different types of learning and one is far more effective than the other.

After the first 100 words, focus on becoming conversational

Studies have shown that the most common 100 words in any language account for 50% of all spoken communication. The most common 1,000 words account for 80% of all spoken communication. The most common 3,000 words account for 99% of communication. In other words, there are some serious diminishing returns from learning more vocabulary.

The basic grammar should get you speaking fundamental sentences within a matter of days.

"Where is the restaurant?"

"I want to meet your friend."

"How old is your sister?"

"Did you like the movie?"
The first few hundred words will get you pretty far. Use them to get as comfortable as possible with grammar, idioms, slang and constructing thoughts, jokes, and ideas in the new language on the fly. Once you're able to joke consistently in the new language, that's a pretty good sign that it's time to expand your vocabulary.

A lot of people attempt to expand their vocabulary too quickly and too soon. It's a waste of time and effort because they're still not comfortable with basic conversations about where they're from, yet they're studying vocabulary about economics or medicine. It makes no sense.

Aim for the brain melt

You know how when you do a lot of intellectually-intensive work for hours and hours on end, at some point your brain just feels like a lump of gravy? Shoot for that moment when learning languages. Until you've reached brain-gravy stage, you probably aren't maximizing your time or effort. In the beginning, you'll hit mind-melt within an hour or two. Later on, it may take an entire night of hanging out with locals before it happens. But when it happens, it's a very good thing.

Use the language daily

Unless you have superhuman abilities, you're not going to become fluent in a language if you don't use it often and consistently. And the best way to ensure you hit both marks is simply to use it daily. Keep having those mental monologues.

Go over those 100 words and conversational phrases you learned so they stick. Better yet, immerse yourself in the new language. Changing the operating language on your browser or phone will leave you disoriented for a few days, but it will get you used to seeing the language in your daily life. Listen to podcasts or the radio in your target language on your commute.

Watch YouTube videos in the language you're trying to learn. A lot of foreign-language videos will have English subtitles. And if you're feeling bold, you can even watch them without the subtitles! The Internet is your friend. Let it help you melt your brain every day.

"How do you say X?" is the most important sentence you can possibly learn

Learn it early and use it often.

One-on-one tutoring is the best and most efficient use of time

It's also usually the most expensive use of time, depending on the language and country. But if you have the money, grabbing a solid tutor and sitting with him or her for a few hours every day is the fastest way to learn a new language
However, there are alternatives. Speaking of which...

Date someone who speaks the target language and not your native language

Talk about investment and motivation. You'll be fluent in a month. And best of all, if you annoy them or do something wrong, you can claim that it was lost in translation.

If you can't find someone cute who will put up with you, find a language buddy online

There are a number of websites of foreigners who want to learn English who would be willing to trade practice time in their native language for practice in yours. Here is an overview (https://bilingua.io/best-language-exchange-apps-websites) of language exchange websites and apps. (The reviews are written by Bilingua, which is itself one of the apps reviewed, so take their bias into account.)

Facebook chat + Google Translate = Win Win

Seriously, technology is amazing. Use it.

When you learn a new word, try to use it a few times right away

When you stop and look up a new word in conversation, make a point to use it in the next two or three sentences you say. Language learning studies show that you need to hit a certain amount of repetitions of saying a word within one minute of learning it, one hour of learning it, one day, etc. Try to use it immediately a few times and then use it again later in the day. Chances are it'll stick.

TV shows, movies, newspapers and magazines are good supplements

But they should not be mistaken or act as replacements for legitimate practice. It is good to watch a couple movies each week and read a newspaper article each day in your TL. It's helpful to keep you fresh, but it is not as helpful as time spent in conversation.

Most people are helpful, let them help

If you're in a foreign country and making a complete ass out of yourself trying to buy something at the grocery store, ask random people for help. Point to something and ask how to say it. Ask them questions. Most people are friendly and willing to help you out. Learning a language is not for shy people.

There will be a lot of ambiguity and miscommunication

Fact of the matter is that for many, many words, the translations are not direct. "Gustar" may roughly mean "to like" in Spanish, but in usage, it's more nuanced than that. It's used for particular situations and contexts, whereas in English we use "like" as a blanket verb covering anything we enjoy or care about. These subtle differences can add up, particularly in serious or emotional conversations.

Intentions can be easily misconstrued. Nuanced conversations over important matters will likely require double the effort to nail down the exact meaning for each person than it would between two native speakers. No matter how good you are in your new language, you're not likely to have a complete grasp over the slight intuitive differences between each word, phrase or idiom that a native speaker does without living in the country for years.

These are the phases you go through

First, you're able to speak a little and understand nothing. Then you're able to understand far more than you speak. Then you become conversational, but it requires quite a bit of mental effort. After that, you're able to speak and understand without conscious mental effort (i.e., you don't have to translate words into your native tongue in your mind). Once you're able to speak and listen without thinking about it, you'll begin to actually think in the foreign language itself without effort. Once this happens, you're really hitting a high level.

And the final level? Believe it or not, being able to follow a conversation between a large group of native speakers is the last piece of the puzzle to fall into place. Or at least it was for me. Once that happens, and you're able to interject, come in and out of the conversation at will, you're pretty set. After that, there's not really anywhere else to go without living in the country for at least a year or two and reaching complete fluency.

Finally, find a way to make it fun

As with anything, if you're going to stick to it, you have to find a way to make it fun. Find people you enjoy talking to. Go to events where you can practice while doing something fun. Don't just sit in a classroom in front of a book, or you're likely to burn out fairly quickly. Talk about personal topics which you care about. Find out about the person you're talking to. Make it personal, a life experience, or else you're going to be in for a long, unenjoyable process which will likely end up in you forgetting everything you learned.

Once you have mastered a language to your satisfaction don't let your linguistic journey end there. There are many other languages to learn and enjoy and it gets easier with each one.

It's only a short step...

Made in the USA
Coppell, TX
27 March 2025

47631212R00059